STILL DADDY'S GIRL

D. Morgan

HARVEST HOUSE PUBLISHERS

EUGENE, OREGON

Still Daddy's Girl

Text copyright © 2002 by Doris Morgan

Published by Harvest House Publishers
Eugene, Oregon 97402

Library of Congress Cataloging-in-Publication Data

ISBN 0-7369-0522-7

To learn more about the D. Morgan collector's club or to locate a preferred dealer near you, please contact her exclusive print publisher and distributor, Cottage Garden Collections, toll free 1-877-210-3456.

Design and production by Koechel Peterson and Associates, Minneapolis, Minnesota

Printed in China

02 03 04 05 06 07 08 09 10 11 /IM / 10 9 8 7 6 5 4 3 2 1

Make the moments matter
For the memories you give —
Will be with them
Forever ...

...As long
As they
May
Live.

Dear
Daddy, Thanks for
The Memories,

The shoulder always there,
The strong and tender care.
With God our guide
And you beside—
Made hard times unaware...

I thank
You
So
Much.

D. Morgan © 1998

Dedication

Daddy

For all your lessons of life, and for all our hard times too, I will always be grateful to you.

You taught me to see with new eyes, to believe in things unseen, to listen and ponder all of God's smallest wonders.

Remembering your sense of humor, your infinite patience, your wisdom and your endearing love, you are with me, here, in my heart always.

How else would I have learned the words and music to "Bullfrog Sittin' on a Lily Pad," how to enjoy fried salt mackerel, where doodlebugs live, and how to lay a hardwood floor with a finished surface as smooth as marble?

By the time I was eight years old, you had introduced me to works by Victor Hugo, Charlie Chaplain, and the legitimate theater. You had taught me how to find sweet shrub, to fly a

June bug on a string, and that life without music would be like life without love.

You taught me how to paint.

Daddy, I still feel safe and warm thinking of you. You left me a legacy of memories I will cherish forever. And so, to my keeper of dreams, John Lovic Whitten, country gentleman of many talents, to you, Daddy, with all my love, I dedicate this book.

Mother

With loving and fitting tribute to Cornelia Slater Whitten, who, at ninety-six years old in the year 2001, continues to endear herself to everyone with her quick wit, Southern charm, and timeless beauty. With her astonishing capacity to embrace life to the fullest, she has truly found her fountain of youth.

And so, with love to my mother, Daddy's wife...truly the girl of his dreams, this book is also dedicated to you.

A DIFFERENT Time

Growing up in the forties was a different time. I cherish those childhood memories. It was a time before children carried guns and used drugs. It was a magical time when imagination was stimulated by listening to the radio, reading wonderful books, and making a fort from a large cardboard box. Our experiences through life mold and make us who we are. I had the good fortune of spending a great deal of time with my dad. He had the wit of Chaplin, the soul of an artist, the heart of a lion, and the patience of Job. We were soul mates. There are special people in our lives who never leave us, even after they are gone.

Seldom an evening has ended

Rarely a new
day begins
That I don't think
about you ~
Good times ~
True loves ~
Old
Friends.

D. Morgan © 1993

The music plays,
THE HEART REMEMBERS...

...And

The
MELODY
Lingers
On.

LINGER LONGER IN THE SUNSET,
Walk barefoot in the rain.
This path of light—
This state of mind
WILL NOT PASS THIS WAY AGAIN.

My tears become rainbows
When…
I
Remember
You.

Through the pines
The light that shines
Greets me like a friend.
Happy hours beckon...

D. Morgan

Home
Is
Just
Around
the
Bend.

Supper's on the stove.
THERE ARE PLACES SET FOR THREE.

I want to go inside and find them
Waiting
There
for
Me.
Through kitchen
windows in the night,
When lamps are lit
And burning bright—
I feel that warmth
of long ago
From windows
I don't
Even
Know.

A light in the kitchen window

Finds me yesterday's
Best friend—
And sweet memories surface
To
Take
Me
HOME
AGAIN.

Ol' BILL

Our family dog Ol' Bill was undeniably Daddy's best friend and constant companion for 21 years. Through mere glance and body language, they communed. Through all his years, Bill's outdoor life included death-defying confrontations and encounters—from skunk spray to snake bite—but was always laced with an abundance of love.

Bill's custom-built house, with blankets he could puff and paw like pampas grass, was just right for him. On especially cold nights, Daddy insisted Ol' Bill come inside to sleep in the warm kitchen. After a number of enticing invitations, Bill would reluctantly enter his master's house with bowed head and apologetic demeanor. He then slept serenely by the fire, feeling warm and dry, but perhaps a bit out of place.

After 21 years, Daddy painfully acknowledged that Bill's time had come. He and Dr. Von Gremp helped Bill pass from this world to the next.

Even now, some 40 years later, at family gatherings we continue to relate stories of Ol' Bill. He was a truly irreplaceable friend.

f all good times remembered
When I was
very young,

My heart
holds most dear...

..The time
My Daddy spent with me.

©1989 D. Morgan

I knew sweet country mornings then.

White leghorn's crow made them begin.
Fresh cut grass and clover chains
    Were painted greener
       With
         the
           Rains.

The yellow sun sometimes set late,
    To grow long shadows from the gate.
I waded barefoot in the stream,
    When milk was topped with yellow cream.

On days when summer rains slept late,
    I'd picnic from my luncheon plate.
In winter, Daddy cut the tree
    And strung the Christmas lights for me.

My heroes wore the hats in white,
And good guys entered from stage right.
I knew sweet country mornings then—
    White leghorn's crow
      Made
       Them
        Begin.

D. Morgan

A PATH OF
Ribbons

Daddy cut that pretty little pine out back. Pulling the tree, we walked toward the house singing our funny songs.

The tree made a path of ribbons in the snow.

Mother had all the Christmas decorations unpacked and ready. The aromas from the kitchen mingled with the freshly cut pine, and after supper the three of us trimmed the tree. We were careful handling the clunky lights. If one went out, so did they all. Some ornaments were shaped like stars, some like icicles, and there were those like winter houses with colored cellophane windows. All were topped with white and silver sparkling glitter that shed under the tree. When the lights caught the tiny dots, they flashed like diamonds.

From my bed, I watched the silent snow drift by my window. Sleep came as the lights grew dim, then dark.

Each December I think of that day into evening and hold most dear to my heart that beautiful Christmas memory.

I'm Dreaming of A White Christmas

A snowy night
A cozy room.
Yuletide holiday in bloom.
The feast, the fun, all play a part
For keeping Christmas . . .
In my heart.
D. Morgan ©

D. Morgan ©1997

Home
IN MY
Heart

I close my eyes and see the old house. I remember where everything was placed. In my favorite room, the kitchen, places are set for supper.

As I come home in my heart, the earth content with pumpkin colors, I feel winter coming all around. I cherish the winter memories most of all—that safe, warm feeling with the hot water bottle wrapped in a blanket at my feet in my winter bed.

But the house is gone. My bedroom window is gone. There is no apple tree, and Puddy's marker is nowhere to be found. Now, the sun still rises each morning and persimmons still wait for the frost. I ponder these things, the real stuff of life. I am so grateful to God who allows me these remembered contentments to fortify my life today and to validate the many treasures of my heart in each and every day He has planned for me.

*We spoke of gypsies,
world affairs,*

OF FICTION, FACT, AND FABLE—

*Of Poe and Frost,
Paradise Lost—
No other Rhett but Gable.
We shared our failures,
Hopes and dreams…*

Around
the
Kitchen
Table.

Trains were here just yesterday—

Or was it long ago?
The tracks are hidden now
Beneath a place
Wildflowers
Grow.

Silver goblets and white linen
Graced the dining car
And porters with their shiny hats
Asked
Were we
Traveling far?

My dolly wore a scarlet ribbon
And proper dress for tea.
White gloves and patent leather
With dotted Swiss for me.

Now, when I hear that whistle blow
I still remember when...
Once the world was full of trains,
But the
World
Was
Younger
Then.

My HOMETOWN

There were many pleasant houses on the wide, shady street. Magnolia, oak, and poplar trees grew all around our house. But the chinaberry trees, with their limbs close to the ground, were best for climbing. The fragrance of honeysuckle was intoxicating.

On the small town square, birds fluttered amid the knobs and carvings of the old courthouse. Across the street, Tatum's drugstore soda fountain served a delicious concoction of lemon, lime, and Lithia water.

It was a different world when gentle people took time to enjoy the simple pleasures of gracious living.

I can see Daddy with arms full of new puppies and hear Mother singing in the kitchen. And for one fleeting moment—I am a child again.

I cherish all

I her

...mories...

..... Of every sight and sound

...rong the gentle people

Back in my home town.

D. Morgan © 1996

There the home fires
BURNING BRIGHT

Warmed me on a winter's night.
  Honeysuckle on the vine,
Pickled watermelon rind.
  Crickets on a summer night,
A pilgrimage of birds in flight.
  Wading barefoot in a stream
Sleeping through a favorite dream.
  Purple cane at Crowley's store,
That felt fedora Daddy wore.
  Popcorn,
    Ponies,
      Yellow roses,
Newborn puppies
  With wet noses.
Courthouse squares
  With bell clock towers,
Walking on the beach for hours.
  Standing tall,
    First snowfall,
Horseback rides down country lanes,
  Thunderstorms—summer rains.

Country gardens
  Gentle faces
Cozy little wayside places.
  Being kind to all God's creatures,
Saturday movie double features.
So many things
  My memory traces—
    All of these
      My
        Heart
          Embraces.

Always in April . . . . All through December . . .
. . . Those were the times I love
To
Remember.

D. Morgan © 1978

The SUNDAY SCHOOL Teacher

Miss Opie Davis, Daddy's Sunday school teacher, had spent the better part of her life teaching school and Sunday school in Harris county during the early 1900s. Daddy spoke of Miss Opie in endearing terms throughout his life.

Her house commanded a grand view, and its walls held generations of memories.

In her later years at social gatherings, she and the other older womenfolk would sit in the wicker rockers on the veranda, wearing shawls against the late afternoon chill. They would enjoy their tea and cakes while holding a requiem for their youth.

Changing Times
Changing paces

Parents, Children
Changing places.

Winning, Losing
Loving Faces—
Leaving us with
Empty
Spaces.

Others may treasure untold wealth ~ mansions, diamonds, rubies and gold. ~ But richer than I they will never be...... I had a Dad who spent time with me.

Daddy's
MOTHER

A covey of birds whooshed close to my head,
then stillness. The sound of silence was
broken by the voice of Daddy's mother softly
singing, "There's power in the blood." The
photograph of my grandmother Danny at
eighteen rushed through my memory—a
proper Victorian lady then—long gone. It
was a time of gracious living, simple pleasures,
and gentle people.

I'm just a bit old fashioned.
I believe in good and simple things.
Prayer in school,
The golden rule
Love and wedding rings.

I believe in
The handshake seal
That heaven's real
Lingering in sunsets longer
Broken hearts mending stronger
The Disney way.
A better day.

I still believe in ~
Santa Claus,
And the wonderful Wizard of Oz.
I do.
Believe.

You too?

MEMORIES IN THE MIST,

take me

home

again.

D. Morgan © 1997

THE GLOW OF EARLY EVENING

Soft as lantern light—
Purple shadows falling
Like a
    Fragile
      Paper
        Kite.

Yesterday's Style And Grace
Another time — another
It was real — a drea
Bear Creek

D. Morgan

THE AIR IS CRISP AS APPLES,

Hurried steps are light—
And in the sound of silence,
There is
Magic
in
the
Night.

I'll build my home
WITHIN A TREE—

And live my childhood fantasy.
   The leafy branches wet with rain
Would dance against my windowpane.

My change of season home would wear
   A springtime garland in her hair.
Then wild with crimson dress for fall—
   And in winter with no clothes at all.

Upon the sturdy limbs, a stair
   To climb the many stories there.
I'll count the stars just overhead
   As I stumble into bed.

All would be well with world and me—
   In my home…
      Within
        a
          Tree.

You beautiful old tree—

I lay at your trunk
And look above—
Wearing flowers in your hair

You're like a
Schoolgirl in love...

Daddy's PAIN

For the first and last time, Daddy went hunting with his older brothers, at their insistence. He held his breath as he pulled the trigger—and watched the little bird in death. Daddy was nine. Remembering the limping flight was a childhood memory hard to bear. That pain he felt is also mine.

.....Where the water meets the mount[e]

I never knew that paradise on earth was so nearby....

And the mountains meet the sky.

Our legacy is left

In the footprints...

...That

We

Leave.

My cup is full,
I've found my way—

The fruit is on the vine.

I will not waste this precious day

For it is...

Truly

Mine.

There's a little bit of heaven

'Round the corner,
Take a right…
A cozy little cottage
With a little
Kitchen
Light.

Bless this house,

Dear Lord, we pray—
Be with us each night
And day.
With each new morning,
Come what may;

Thank heaven
You're just
A
Prayer
Away

Start each day believing

You will find…
A
Little
Magic.
It was springtime—
Life was sweet—
And we were very young.

little child just yesterday was here at home

now grown away

Those wonder years too sweet to last
Are now dear memories of the past.

Now let's make new dreams
Come true.

Doing things
We've planned to do.

Sweetly, sadly, swiftly...
Seasons go.

I have his cup, my Daddy's cup,

Cracked and worn
    Across the rim.
His favorite book—the book of books,
    Whose pages
        Now are dim.
You could not buy them from me
With all the world's most precious gems.

If you hear a different drummer — dream

...The road you choose to trav

Means the differ

He was the
Keeper
of
Dreams.

But I would gladly give them
For one more
Day
With
Him.

a chance ...

On The Dance.

D. Morgan ©1998

There'll be no good-byes for us—
DADDY, DEAREST FRIEND.

BEYOND THE BLUE HORIZON...

We

Will

Meet

Again.

About
THE AUTHOR

Doris Whitten Morgan is a fourth-generation native of Atlanta, Georgia. She studied art formally at the High Museum School of Art in Atlanta, but continues to credit her dad, the late John Lovic Whitten, as her most influential teacher. Doris began showing her work at sidewalk shows in 1972. Today she is one of the most popular published artists in America. You will find Doris's work featured in gift shops, galleries, mail order catalogs, and on many licensed products.

With paint and pen, D. Morgan has fashioned her God-given gift into her own unique style. Many of her emotions form the foundation for her inspirational messages. Because we have all experienced some of the same joy and pain in life, a special bond is formed with the artist. For in one way or another, D. Morgan has truly touched our hearts.